S0-AUT-120

Stories of Call

Saying Yes to God in Everyday Life

By Phil Haslanger

HI-TIME PUBLISHING Corp.

Artwork and Design — Elizabeth A. Robbins-Ptak

Photo Credits
Richard F. Bauer — page 61
Bright Family Album — page 44
The Christian Science Monitor/Neal Menschel — page 33
Jack Hamilton — page 47
Phil Haslanger — pages 13, 21, 41, 52
NC News Service — pages 30, 58
Sunrise-Trinity — page 38
The Crosiers/Gene Plaisted — page 10

Published with Ecclesiastical Permission.

Volume 17

Focus on HOPE, a series of adult education courses, with a **Guide for the Discussion Leader** available for each course, is published by HI-TIME Publishing Corp. Mailing address: Box 13337, Milwaukee, WI 53213. Subscription in bulk (5 or more copies of one course sent to one address) $2.45 per copy. With a bulk order, the **Guide for the Discussion Leader** is available at $1.25 per copy. Single orders: $4.90 per copy of **Focus on HOPE,** $3.75 per copy of the **Guide for the Discussion Leader.** (Please write for foreign rates.)

Scripture texts used in this work are taken from THE NEW AMERICAN BIBLE, with Revised New Testament, copyright © 1986, by the Confraternity of Christian Doctrine, Washington, DC, and are used with permission. All rights reserved.

Copyright © 1988, HI-TIME Publishing Corp.

All rights reserved, which includes the right to reproduce this publication or portions thereof in any form whatsoever.

Library of Congress Catalog Card Number 88-82297

ISBN 0-937997-10-2

Stories of Call

By Phil Haslanger

Contents

FOCUS ON
HOPE

STORIES OF CALL is one in a series of courses for adult religious education and small-group discussion. Each course presents contemporary Church teaching in a clear and informative style with challenging questions for personal reflection and group discussion. A **Guide for the Discussion Leader** is also available.

Author

Phil Haslanger is an associate editor of *The Capital Times* in Madison, Wisconsin. He has worked for that daily newspaper since 1973, covering politics, education, and religion. For five years he was the city editor, and now he writes the paper's editorials and directs its opinion sections. He is a graduate of the University of Wisconsin–Madison, where he majored in sociology and later received a master degree in journalism.

He spent a year on the program staff at the University Catholic Center in Madison, and a year on the board of directors of the Madison Urban Ministry. He has also worked with couples preparing for marriage, given talks at parish programs, and worked with a parish group organizing a meal program for those in need. He and his wife have conducted workshops for couples entering second marriages.

The Haslangers have four children.

 **Introduction**

The sun was shining warmly on Sandy Simonson's front yard as we sat and talked that morning in June. Sandy, a forty-four-year-old widow, was talking about the work she does with farm families in distress. I asked her how she got involved in this work, and she told a story that unnerved me.

It was as if a voice in the night had spoken to her, she said. "Go and start support groups" was the message that kept repeating itself in her brain as she drove from Iowa to Wisconsin late in 1985. She described hearing this message as a religious experience.

A voice in the night? A real sense of calling from God? What is going on here?

I was on a journey that summer. As part of my assignment for *The Capital Times*, the Madison newspaper where I work, I was traveling around Wisconsin doing a series of stories about people who were working to make a difference in the lives of others. At each stop along the way, I asked the same question I asked Sandy: How did you get involved in this? What struck me in the answers was how often religious values and even specific religious experiences had played a central role.

I'm not sure why that surprised me so much. I grew up in a strongly religious family. Religious values have been important for me in a variety of personal, family, and work decisions. I spend a fair amount of time thinking about where I fit in God's universe and how I can better mesh my values with my daily life.

Still, the people I met on that journey helped me focus in a new way on the issue of call. I began to note differences in the ways people discern and respond to God's message. I began to reflect on the theme of call in Scripture. I talked with people who were trying to figure out directions for their lives. And I discovered that I was not alone in my wondering.

The people who conduct the Gallup poll were wondering the same thing. In 1986 they surveyed 1,013 Americans about the role God plays in their decision making. Sixty-nine percent of those surveyed said they believed that God had led or guided them in making a decision. That means that roughly two-thirds of all Americans have some sense of paying attention to God's call.

How does God communicate to you? the survey asked. People could choose as many responses as they believed were appropriate. More than one in three (36 percent) said God had spoken directly to them. Some 39 percent said God spoke through other people. Nearly half (48 percent) said they believed God spoke through their own internal feelings and impressions. Nearly half (49 percent) said God spoke through the Bible.[1]

Questions for Reflection

Pause for a moment. Think about how God works in your life.

- How does God communicate to you?
- Do you know people who believe that what they do is a response to a call from God? How does that sense of call affect their lives?
- How does a sense of call affect your life?

The people who responded to the Gallup survey said they believe that God communicates less directly with people today than He did in biblical times. Maybe that's because some of the biblical stories seem so dramatic.

Isaiah tells of a vision in which God is on a throne and giant angels hover over Him. Their song shakes the doorframe, and smoke fills the house. Then one angel flies down to Isaiah and touches his mouth with an ember the angel has taken from the altar. "Whom shall I send?" God asks. "Who will go for us?" Isaiah wastes no time responding, "Here I am; send me!" And God tells him what to say to the people. (See Isaiah 6:1-10.)

There are no shaking houses nor burning embers in this series of stories. These stories are much closer to our daily experiences, yet they are still stories of call. Some are stories from Scripture. Some are stories of well-known people from this century. Some are the stories of people I met on my journey.

What I tried to do was sort out the ways people discern God's call. None of these ways are mutually exclusive, and you will notice that for many people the ways overlap. Life, after all, doesn't always fit into tidy categories.

The notion of call, of vocation, is an old one. It can have many meanings. It can be a call to a religious conversion or a call to a particular life-style. It can be a way of seeking salvation or it can be a call to prayer. In these stories, I am largely focusing on calls to action, on people who do things to make a difference in the lives of others.

It is worth noting that there is no foolproof method any of these people had for discerning that call. They followed the path that made the most sense to them, whether they were led by the books they read, by the people they met, or by special moments in their lives.

There is an advantage, I think, in focusing on the process of call for these people. Their stories at first may seem beyond our reach. How can we ever be a Martin Luther King or a Dorothy Day or a Thomas Merton? Yet by looking at how they began, by considering their doubts, by looking at the struggles of people from Scripture and people from our own time, we can discover that we are not very far removed from their stories.

The key for them — and the key for us — is a willingness to struggle with the call and then a willingness to be faithful to it.

So these, then, are stories of that struggle. They are stories of God's call and our response.

Questions for Reflection

Before you begin these stories, think back on your own life again.

- Were there special moments when you felt God's presence?
- Were there people or experiences that changed your life?
  Make a note of them now; then come back and look at those experiences again after you have read through these stories.

---

[1]"Beliefs About Ways God Speaks to People," poll conducted by The Gallup Organization, Inc., for the Christian Broadcasting Network, Inc. Interview dates: February 3-17, 1986. Published October 1986. Excerpts used with permission.

One

A Voice
in the Night

It was rare for Yahweh to speak in those days. Visions were uncommon.

They were days not unlike our own. But in the night, a young man named Samuel learned about the power of God's call.

Samuel had been given to the priest, Eli, by his mother, Hannah. This was to fulfill a promise she had made to God if He would only enable her to conceive a child. Samuel was that child, and so she gave him to Eli. This act of faith may have been good for Hannah, who subsequently gave birth to three more sons and two daughters, but it posed some problems for Samuel.

Eli's own two sons knew they had a good thing going. When people brought their sacrifices to the temple at Shiloh, Eli's sons would demand the best of the meat. They used their position to get sexual favors from the women who served at the entry of the meeting tent. Despite pleas from their father that they change their ways, they continued to exploit the people of Israel.

Samuel, meanwhile, was respected by those who came to the temple at Shiloh. He was growing into a fine young man. Now he faced a call to a hard task.

The call came in the night. He heard a voice. "Here I am," Samuel answered, thinking he was talking to Eli. Samuel got up and went into the next room where Eli was sleeping. "Here I am. You called me," he said.

"I did not call you. Go back to sleep," Eli told the young man. A puzzled Samuel went back to his place.

9

Some calls come gently in the night.

Again Samuel heard the voice. "Here I am," he said, rising again and going to Eli. "I did not call you, my son," Eli answered. "Go back to sleep."

Samuel was more puzzled now. Why was he hearing voices? Was somebody playing a trick on him? He went back to his place. Once more, he heard the voice. Once more he got up and went to Eli. "Here I am. You called me," Samuel said.

At last Eli figured out what was going on. So he said to Samuel, "Go to sleep, and if you are called, reply, 'Speak, Lord, for your servant is listening.' "

Now Samuel lay in his place nervous with anticipation. What was happening? What did it mean?

"Samuel, Samuel!" the voice called out.

"Speak, for your servant is listening," Samuel replied.

And then God told Samuel what would happen to Eli and his sons: ". . . I am condemning his family once and for all, because of this crime: though he knew his sons were blaspheming God, he did not reprove them."

This time, Samuel stayed put. He was not anxious to bring such a grim message to the man who had raised him from infancy, to a man who was now going blind and who had agonized over the misdeeds of his sons.

But Eli knew there was a message for him in Samuel's vision. "Hide nothing from me!" he ordered Samuel the next morning. And so Samuel told Eli the message of God, and Eli answered, "He is the Lord. He will do what he judges best."

And then, in the words of the Hebrew Scriptures (Old Testament), "Samuel grew up, and the Lord was with him, not permitting any word of his to be without effect." As for Eli, he died on the day he learned his two sons had been killed in battle. (See 1 Samuel 1-4.)

A voice in the night. That is a common theme in the Bible. Samuel hears a voice and puzzles over its meaning. Joseph, son of Jacob, listens to his dreams and also helps others understand the stories from their subconscious minds. Daniel interprets dreams for the king.

The quiet of the night, the darkness of the sky, the sparkling of the stars or the glimmer of a candle — they all create an atmosphere for introspection. It is in this atmosphere that a person can find direction from the spirit within or from the presence of God without.

Samuel's call came gently in the night. So did Sandra Simonson's.

Sandra grew up on a three-hundred-acre farm near Black River Falls, Wisconsin, about forty miles east of the Mississippi River. When she married, she and her husband Glenn lived and worked on the farm. It wasn't an easy life for Sandra, Glenn, and their five children.

In the course of a few years in the early 1980s:

• A fire destroyed their barn.
• Two of their children developed serious medical problems.
• A hired hand fell off the silo and was killed.
• Some newly purchased cattle were diseased, and they
  infected the rest of the fifty-cow herd.

Then in July, 1984, the hardest blow fell. Glenn was killed in a tractor accident on the farm.

The farm was quiet on the summer day in 1986 that Sandy talked about her life. Most of the animals were gone. The machines were turned off. Within nine months, the farm would be sold at a foreclosure auction.

She was forty-four that summer, a short, vibrant woman who had launched a project designed to help farm families cope with the turmoil of the rural economy. It was the way Sandy turned her grief into hope for others.

Glenn had been killed on a Saturday. The visitation was on the following Monday. Sandy steeled herself to greet the throngs of people she knew would be there. She relied on her faith, on her pastor, and on some favorite words from Scripture to get her through the day. "I made the decision that day that I would be open to the only one who would help me," she said. She latched on to two words, *trust* and *obey*.

One man at the visitation was a colleague of Glenn's from the National Farmers Organization (NFO). The man, who was from Minnesota, had run for the presidency of the NFO. Glenn had given the man a prayer book. At the visitation the man gave the prayer book back to Sandy.

Nearly a year-and-a-half later, Sandy again met the man at an NFO meeting in Des Moines, Iowa. By this time, Sandy had earned an insurance license. She had attended meetings of grief groups. She was trying to go on with her life, yet she was still feeling unsettled.

For Sandra Simonson,
shown here with her son
Mike, God's call came in
the stillness of the night.

At the Des Moines meeting, people Sandy had known through the years pulled her aside to talk about their personal problems. "I realized that it wouldn't make any difference where I go," she recalled. "People realize they can talk to me about very deep personal things."

She had lunch with the man from Minnesota. "He asked me if I ever thought of doing church ministry," she said.

Ideas whirled around in her mind as she drove back through the night toward Wisconsin. "I drove without stopping," Sandy explained. "The message kept repeating itself in my brain: 'Go and start support groups.' "

For Sandy, it was a message from God. "What if I had not obeyed?" she wonders now. But she followed the call. She trusted that God would see her through. Within two months, she had funding from Lutheran Social Services to start support groups for farmers in crisis. In between support group meetings, she spends time with individual farmers who need someone to talk to.

Sandra Simonson's voice in the night gave meaning and direction to her life. It propelled her into a life of service.

Martin Luther King's voice in the night confirmed a life of service — and of risk.

The night was January 27, 1956. King was twenty-six years old. He was leading the boycott of the Montgomery, Alabama, bus system. The white power structure was reacting with outrage. Day after day there were threatening phone calls to him, his wife, and their daughter. He began to hear stories of serious plotting against his life.

On that January night, he had gone to bed and was starting to doze off when the telephone rang. A hate-filled voice said, "Listen, nigger, we've taken all we want from you; before next week you'll be sorry you ever came to Montgomery."

King hung up the phone but could not sleep. "It seemed that all of my fears had come down on me at once," he wrote in *Stride Toward Freedom*, his book about the Montgomery boycott. "I had reached the saturation point."[1]

When Martin Luther King heard
God's call, his political activism
became a spiritual mission.

He paced the floor for a while, then went to the kitchen and made a cup of coffee, but it sat in front of him untouched. He was ready to give up. He was looking for a way out. He tells the story this way:

"In this state of exhaustion, when my courage had all but gone, I decided to take my problem to God. With my head in my hands, I bowed over the kitchen table and prayed aloud. The words I spoke to God that night are still vivid in my memory. 'I am taking a stand for what I believe is right. But now I am afraid . . . I have nothing left. I've come to the point where I can't face it alone.'

"At that moment I experienced the presence of the Divine as I had never experienced Him before. It seemed as though I could hear the quiet assurance of an inner voice saying, 'Stand up for righteousness, stand up for truth; and God will be at your side forever.' Almost at once, my fears began to go. My uncertainty disappeared. I was ready to face anything."[2]

Three nights later, King's home was bombed, although no one was injured. He drew on the strength of his night in the kitchen and faced the terror with calm. He successfully pleaded with an angry black crowd to put away their weapons, urging them to "meet hate with love."[3]

In his biography of King, *Bearing the Cross*, David J. Garrow describes that night in the kitchen as the most important moment in King's life. It was at that point, Garrow said, that King's political activism was transformed into a spiritual mission.

Three different nights. Three different people. Yet all three took seriously the nocturnal stirrings in their souls, and those stirrings transformed their lives.

Night, then, can be a time of calling. In our dreams, in our pacing the floors, when we're on the highway or at the kitchen table, we can experience God's call — if we bring to those moments our unease and uncertainty and then listen for the sense of direction God brings forth from within us.

It may not happen when we expect it. Samuel slept many nights in his place in the temple. Sandy Simonson drove over country roads on other nights. Martin Luther King had innumerable cups of coffee at his kitchen table. But all three persons were able to stand back and listen when the critical night came.

16

Questions for Reflection

Think for a few moments about night.

- If you pray at bedtime, is that a time when you can feel God's presence in a special way?
- Do your dreams sometimes help you find new insights in your life?
- Do you wake during the night, troubled by some aspect of your life, only to find comfort in prayer?
- Might God be speaking to you in the night? Or do you find God in some other fashion?

The stories in succeeding chapters will explore other ways in which God may be speaking to us.

[1]King, Martin Luther, *Stride Toward Freedom*. New York: Harper and Row, Inc., 1958. Excerpts used with permission.
[2]Ibid.
[3]Ibid.

Two

Lightning Strikes

It was noon. Saul of Tarsus was on his way to Damascus to arrest and bring to Jerusalem "any men or women who belonged to the Way" (Acts of the Apostles 9:2; 22:6).

No story of call is more dramatic than this one.

Saul had been making a name for himself by rounding up Christians. "I imprisoned many of the holy ones with the authorization I received from the chief priests," he later told King Agrippa and Bernice, the king's sister. He continued, ". . . and when they were to be put to death I cast my vote against them. Many times, in synagogue after synagogue, I punished them in an attempt to force them to blaspheme; I was so enraged against them that I pursued them even to foreign cities" (Acts 26:10-11).

But on this trip to Damascus, Saul was jolted into a new way of life. A bright light flashed in the sky and Saul fell to the ground. "Saul, Saul, why are you persecuting me?" a voice asked (Acts 9:4). Saul had encountered Jesus. The encounter blinded Saul, and for three days he could not see, he did not eat, he did not drink. Then Ananias — a Christian who knew how to listen to God — went to the house where Saul was staying and touched Saul and spoke to him about Jesus. Saul recovered his sight. Saul, also known as Paul, joined the Christians and became one of the great messengers of Jesus. (See Acts of the Apostles 9:1-22; 13:9.)

Not every call is as dramatic as Paul's, of course. But moments of crisis have a way of opening us up to re-examine our lives, to listen a little more closely to the messages God may be sending us. For Paul, change did not come in an instant flash on the road. That only set the stage for a time of reflection as Paul recovered his health and listened to Ananias.

For us, moments of crisis can take many forms: a birth or a death, a job loss or an illness, a fire or an accident. A crisis can be a debilitating moment or a transforming one. But it is not the crisis which defines that; it is our response. God can use moments of crisis to open our hearts. The call can come in ways and times that we least expect.

___

Questions for Reflection

Put yourself in the place of Saul of Tarsus. One day he is the sworn enemy of the Christians. A few days later he is one of them.

- What sort of problems would a 180-degree turn like Paul's cause in your life?
- How would you deal with those problems?

___

La Vella Hawes and Shirley Iaquinta both had every reason in the world to give up. Both were facing death at the prime of their lives. Both felt a call to do more than be invalids. Both became the dynamos who run a neighborhood center in one of the toughest neighborhoods of Kenosha, an economically depressed, blue-collar city in the southeastern corner of Wisconsin.

La Vella is a forty-one-year-old woman whose parents were a black man and an American Indian woman. She grew up in rural Louisiana and Mississippi. She has a degree in sociology, has

Shirley Iaquinta and La Vella Hawes
each faced death and used that
experience to give new meaning
and new direction to their lives.

studied nursing and has studied accounting. She has a fourteen-year-old adopted daughter. She is a Catholic whose religious beliefs run through everything she does.

Shirley, sixty-two, is a white woman who grew up in a relatively poor family in Kenosha. She dropped out of high school to get married, then went back to school to get her Graduate Equivalent Degree (GED) at age forty, with her five children there to cheer for her. She is a Lutheran who spent twenty years teaching Sunday school.

La Vella was twenty-eight when she was in a serious car accident. She was paralyzed. She went through forty-one operations over a five-to-six-year period and eventually recovered her ability to walk.

"In the interim, I came to know God a little better than I knew Him before," she explained. "After eighteen months of hospital confinement, I realized I would never get well unless I could do it myself. My mother taught me I could be and do what I wanted to be. I developed a belief in God and started to pull myself together. I knew I had to do something that would give me meaning."

The neighborhood center she and Shirley started in 1975 helped give her life meaning. It serves about eighty-five new families a month, and La Vella sometimes sleeps there on weekends when the calls for help become too intrusive for her husband and daughter at home.

Evenings and weekends, she uses her nursing skills to help about fifteen elderly people in their homes: giving medication, helping with baths, cleaning the house when cleaning is needed.

She even does funerals, two or three a year. When people with no money and no family die, she does the legwork, getting state approval for burial money, helping at the funeral home to cut costs, even on occasion taking her husband's suits (with his approval, of course) to bury people in.

It may sound as if La Vella has just followed a straight line — she found her mission and went to work. It hasn't been that easy. "Every morning I say, 'Why are you doing this?' " La Vella explained. "I call that wrestling with God." She has found her answer in the success stories of the people she has worked with, in doing something that gives her life meaning, in responding to God's call.

Shirley was forty-nine when she was diagnosed as having a rare muscle inflammation disease. The doctors gave her a year or two to live. She could walk only with great pain and weakness.

But she survived, learned to walk again, and today is healthy. "I felt God had something more for me to do," she said simply.

Now, in Shirley's words, she works with La Vella "to help people understand that you're somebody."

"We're very gutsy ladies," Shirley said at one point. They are gutsy ladies who faced death and used that experience to give new meaning and new direction to their lives.

We don't always respond quickly to God's call, even when we can feel it tugging at us. Sometimes we are skeptical of God's call. Sometimes we try hard to avoid it.

That's what happened to Saul, the king of Israel.

Samuel, having had his own experience with God's call, now was the bearer of the call to Saul. The Israelites were clamoring for a king. You're making a mistake, Samuel warned them. "We too must be like other nations, with a king to rule us and to lead us in warfare and fight our battles," they replied (1 Samuel 8:20). So God decided to let the Israelites have a king, and God chose Saul, described as a "handsome young man" who "stood head and shoulders above the people" (1 Samuel 9:2). Saul, however, didn't know what God had in mind for him. Once he found out, he tried to avoid the call.

Saul was out looking for some lost donkeys and heard that Samuel was a wise man who might offer advice. Saul got more advice than he had hoped for. As Saul was about to leave the town, Samuel poured oil over his head, kissed him and told him, "You are to govern the LORD's people Israel, and to save them from the grasp of their enemies roundabout" (1 Samuel 10:1).

Sensing that Saul was skeptical of this news, Samuel promised Saul three signs on his way home. He would meet two men who would tell him that his father was no longer worried about the donkeys but now was worried about him; he would meet three men carrying goats, bread and wine; and then he would meet a band of prophets playing lyres, tambourines, flutes and harps.

Even after all that happened, Saul still neglected to tell his father about his new job. Seven days later, Samuel called the Israelites together. He picked a tribe from which the ruler would

"Behold, I am the
handmaid of the Lord."

Luke 1:38

come. He drew a lot which indicated that Saul was the king. But Saul was nowhere to be found. He was hiding among the baggage. Over the course of time, Saul accepted his call, consolidated his power and became a strong king. (See 1 Samuel 9-10.)

One of the quickest responses to a call from God came from Mary, the mother of Jesus.

She was a young woman, perhaps just a teenager, who was looking forward to marrying her fiancé, Joseph, a carpenter. Gabriel, a messenger from God, came to her.

"Hail, favored one! The Lord is with you," Gabriel said.

Mary didn't know what to make of this stranger.

"Do not be afraid, Mary," Gabriel re-assured her, "for you have found favor with God. Behold, you will conceive in your womb and bear a son, and you shall name him Jesus."

Mary was still puzzled. She was not yet married. She was a virgin. She did not have, in her words, "relations with a man."

Gabriel explained: "The holy Spirit will come upon you, and the power of the Most High will overshadow you. Therefore the child to be born will be called holy, the Son of God."

He told her that her cousin Elizabeth, who had thought she was sterile, had conceived and was now six months pregnant. That should prove, Gabriel continued, that "nothing will be impossible for God."

Mary waited no longer. "Behold, I am the handmaid of the Lord. May it be done to me according to your word." (See Luke 1:26-38.)

Questions for Reflection

- Are you more like King Saul or more like Mary?
- Do you find yourself trying to avoid God's call or embracing it eagerly? Are there elements of both in your life? What makes the difference?

Not every call is as dramatic as Paul's on the road to Damascus or that of Shirley or La Vella on their sickbeds. Our responses are not always as reluctant as that of King Saul or as quick as that of Mary.

There is a common thread in the stories we have read so far, a thread which offers another way of thinking about the notion of hearing a call. That thread was highlighted most clearly by La Vella Hawes. She knew she had to do something that would give her life meaning.

Answering this question is one way of testing a call: Do you find that this idea gives meaning to your life, or does it seem at odds with who you are and what your talents are? In the stories of the first chapter, the calls answered by Sandra Simonson and Martin Luther King gave a new meaning to the use of their talents. Saul of Tarsus changed his life and found new meaning. Shirley and La Vella embarked on a new effort of helping others and found personal rewards.

What you have here is a mixture of some of the biblical notions of call. God called individuals like David or Aaron or Isaiah or Deborah or Ruth or Miriam not for their own benefit, but for the benefit of the Hebrew community. In the stories of call we have considered so far, the people found personal meaning, but they also did something for society at large.

So if we learn to listen for the gentle call in the night, we must also watch for the flash of light in the day. We must watch for the ways dramatic events in our lives can be moments of call. Put another way, we must look for how those events can give new meaning to our lives and enrich our society.

God, after all, picks different ways to nudge us out of our routines.

Three

A Stranger on the Road

Jesus had just come back from forty days in the desert. His cousin John had baptized Him in the Jordan River, and Jesus had wrestled with the temptations to wealth, power, and fame. Now He was ready to call together the people who would be closest to Him during His public ministry. (See Luke 3:21-22; 4:1-15.)

They were doing the things of everyday life, these men of Galilee. Simon, James, and John were at work fishing. Matthew was busy collecting taxes. Philip met Jesus on the road and then went to bring his friend Nathanael to meet Jesus. Others were called from the crowds that listened to Jesus speak. (See Luke 5:1-11; Matthew 9:9-13; 10:2-3; John 1:45-51.)

No voices in the night here. No bolts out of the blue. Just a one-on-one personal encounter that changed the lives of these people.

So, too, with the women of Galilee. Luke tells us that Jesus drove seven demons out of Mary Magdalene, and that she, along with Joanna and Susanna, was part of Jesus' group of closest followers. (See Luke 8:1-3.) The woman at the well had her life transformed by her meeting with Jesus. Jesus' friends Martha and Mary also experienced the transformation of their lives. (See John 4:7-26; 11:1-44.)

Questions for Reflection

• If you had been Simon or James or John or Mary Magdalene or the woman at the well, how would you have responded to a stranger inviting you to change your life?
• What was it about Jesus' call that attracted these people?

In the stories of call in the Gospels, actions and events seem to happen very quickly. Jesus calls; people respond. Not every call is so clear; not every response, so quick. Yet the people we meet — whether they are strangers in a park or friends who shape our thinking — can be among the most vibrant messengers of God.

In the following two stories, we will see that Dorothy Day, the founder of the Catholic Worker Movement, and Noel Paul Stookey, a member of the Peter, Paul and Mary singing trio, came to their calling in large part through the experiences they had with other people. The strength of someone else's personality and the power of someone else's ideas helped give direction to the lives of these two people in search of a mission. In the case of Dorothy Day, the encounter changed her career as well as her personal life. Noel Paul Stookey stayed in the same career, but his encounter with a stranger changed his life and transformed his music.

*   *   *   *

For Dorothy Day, the call came slowly, over a period of years. It came through her own disquiet and through people who touched her life, especially Peter Maurin.

It was 1917. Dorothy was a nineteen-year-old radical journalist. She was arrested outside the White House with a group of militant suffragists. For six days, she sat alone in a cell, joining the other women in a hunger strike. On the fourth day, one of the guards gave her a Bible. She felt comforted as she read the Book of Psalms, yet guilty that she was relying on religion as a crutch.

Still, she would sometimes find herself in church for early morning Mass after spending all night at a tavern or a dance. She didn't pray, she said later. She just sat in the back, again feeling a vague sense of comfort.

In 1923, she was living for the winter in a room rented from a Catholic family. She would see them kneel to pray. She read the New Testament. The strands were swirling around her, but she had not yet pulled them together.

By the time her daughter, Tamar, was born in 1927, Dorothy knew that she wanted her child baptized in the Catholic Church, even though she knew that her lover — the girl's father — would strongly object. Six months later, in December, 1927, Dorothy, now 30, sought Baptism for herself — a decision that finally ended her relationship with her lover, yet a decision that gave her no clues about her future. She got to know her new Church, concentrated on raising her daughter, and did writing and odd jobs.

In the summer of 1932, she went to Washington, DC, as a free-lance reporter to write about a hunger march. Her story was for *America* and *Commonweal* magazines. It was a moment of crisis for Dorothy. She felt isolated from the marchers and wondered how what they were doing related to her faith. On December 8, she went to the unfinished Shrine of the Immaculate Conception in Washington and prayed "that some way would open up for me to use what talents I possessed for my fellow workers, for the poor."[1]

The night she returned to New York, a man named Peter Maurin was at her door. The editor of *Commonweal* had suggested that Maurin, a fifty-four-year-old French itinerant philosopher, seek out the thirty-five-year-old Dorothy to tell her about his personalist philosophy — the notion that you bring about change through personal acts of commitment and kindness rather than through mass movements. For four months, Maurin came daily to talk to her about the history of the Church and its meaning for contemporary life. He convinced her to use her skills as a journalist to spread his message.

On May 1, 1933, the *Catholic Worker* newspaper was born, and Dorothy Day had found her calling. Subsequently, she helped guide the establishment of some forty Catholic Worker Houses of Hospitality throughout the nation. Over the next forty-seven years, she fed and housed hundreds of thousands of the poor and homeless on New York's Lower East Side. She protested against war

Dorothy Day's call came
through her own restlessness
and through the people
who touched her life.

and hunger, often going to jail for her acts of civil disobedience. Strengthened by a strong traditional Catholic spirituality, she lived a life of personal poverty. Dorothy Day's life and ideas helped shape the social and economic thinking of a whole generation of American Catholics.

She said that through it all, she worked toward the establishment of a society in which people would find it easier to be good. By the time she died at age 83 on November 29, 1980, she had done for many others what Peter Maurin had done for her: help them hear the call of God in their lives.

Questions for Reflection

For a moment, think about your own religious journey.
- If you grew up as a believer, were there people who helped give life and meaning to your faith? If there were, who were they and how did they help?
- If you came to your beliefs later in life, were there people who were an important part of your process of discovery? If there were, who were they and how did they help?
- How have the people in your life affected you with regard to what you believe and how you live?

In the 1960s, an era in which folk music broke into the big commercial markets, Paul Stookey was part of Peter, Paul and Mary, one of the hottest folk music groups. They wove their songs through the lives of a generation, songs ranging from their own "Puff the Magic Dragon" to Bob Dylan's "Blowin' in the Wind" and "The Times They Are A-Changin' " to Pete Seeger's "If I Had a Hammer."

It was a heady time for the three young musicians. They were winning fame, earning big money, and participating in some of the most historic events of the decade — the 1963 Civil Rights March in Washington, civil rights rallies in the South, anti-war protests on college campuses.

For Paul Stookey, it was also a time of searching. He had grown up in Birmingham, Michigan, in a family that was not particularly religious. He describes his father as a "somewhat reluctant ex-Mormon" and his mother as a "nonpracticing Roman Catholic." He went to Michigan State University at Lansing and then headed to New York City by way of a brief stop in Pennsylvania, where he worked in a camera shop. In New York, he got a job with a photographic chemical company by day and began to perform by night at a Greenwich Village pub called The Commons. It was there he met Mary Travers, and soon they began doing sets together at a place called the Gaslight. Mary introduced him to Peter Yarrow and the trio was born.

Religious themes were not uncommon in the trio's folk music in the early 1960s, but Stookey saw them just as part of the folk music tradition. Those songs "were not so much heartfelt as accommodated," he says now. But in the songs he was writing in the mid-1960s, he began to "speak of the search for meaning in my own personal life."

In the meantime, he was reveling in the high life of a famous entertainer — something he now describes as the "success-excess syndrome." He recalls those days: "I had pretty much abused my position as a human being by virtue of having more money and status than I knew how to deal with." Still, he was uneasy with the contradictions between the pastoral themes in the folk songs he was singing and his "living in a million-and-half-dollar house and waking up at 11:00 a.m. after having champagne and strawberries the night before."

Then the stranger appeared in Paul's life.

It was at a concert in Texas in 1968. A young man in his early twenties was standing backstage at intermission. He asked Paul if they could talk. This was an era when many young men approached members of the trio to talk about dealing with the military draft. So when the young man — his name was Steve — asked for some of Paul's time, Paul thought, Sure, I'll help you out, kid.

Paul tells what happened next: "When I saw him after the show, I said, 'What is it you'd like to talk to me about?' He got me right full in the eyes. He said, 'I want to talk to you about God.' You know that funny feeling you get when you run into an expert. I knew the guy was speaking from experience. I'm really thankful that my parents raised me to trust someone until they prove themselves otherwise."

Paul told Steve he had to sign some autographs, but that he'd listen to him. "It didn't phase the guy at all," Paul continues. "I'm

© The Christian Science Monitor/Neal Menschel

For Noel Paul Stookey, God's
call came through a stranger.
It led him to live a simpler
life and to write and record
deeply religious songs.

signing autographs, and he's telling me his life story. I'm fascinated. He's talking about how, through the dramatic intervention of the Holy Spirit, he now has a personal relationship with Jesus Christ and what that means. I kept drawing connections between what I was looking for in my life and what had happened in his life."

Steve and some of his friends went back to Paul's hotel room with him. "I made a few feeble attempts to establish the credibility of my own spiritual search," Paul recalls, "like asking him about re-incarnation and some other qualifiers to impress upon him that I had done some reading." But Paul soon found that he was out of his league. He listened, captivated by the young man's story.

"When the opportunity came to talk directly to God in a prayerful position, I just started to cry," Paul says. "I realized at that moment, as I said I was sorry, that I was confessing not only a distance from God, but confessing all the excesses of my life as well. The following morning, I was a new person. But even so, I had had enough parties and smoked enough dope and been in enough circumstances that as I walked out of the room and glanced back at it, I thought: I wonder if this is one of those things that's going to fade away or whether the experience of last night — which was very powerful — will continue."

Continue it did, transforming every aspect of Paul's life. He changed his name to Noel Paul Stookey. He and his family moved from their urban house to a place in the Maine countryside. He began to write songs with explicit religious themes, the most notable of which may have been "The Wedding Song." He talked on stage about his conversion. And he found that the Peter, Paul and Mary audiences were unnerved. "The name of Jesus has incredible impact in terms of sorting people into their assessment of how their lives relate to that name," he says now. The audience began to fractionalize; tensions in the trio were growing. Finally, in the early 1970s, Peter, Paul and Mary decided to take some time apart. It was seven years before they were re-united. In the meantime, Paul began to work with his own musical group, Bodyworks, to write and record songs that were more explicitly religious.

"I'm surprised and blessed that God has held me away from the mainstream," he reflects now. "There were lots of opportunities to collapse into the system either as a pop writer or a pop performer. But folk music was a thread for me that connected real life and my musical career. Folk music, in a sense, demands a responsibility and says your life and this music are connected."

Sometimes that leaves him isolated. His religious songs — except for "The Wedding Song" — never hit mainstream radio, but they are not part of the Christian pop music world, either. "I am part of a small group of believers who find themselves much more liberal than the mainstream evangelicals, yet represent an increasing number of concerned Christians who see a need to connect the integrity of their faith with the integrity of their lives."

So he sings about bloodshed in El Salvador. He traveled to the Philippines with the trio to support the nonviolent revolution there. He faced arrest outside the South African embassy. His encounter with a stranger — and with God — filled in the meaning in his life and gave new depth to his work and his commitments to peace and justice.

"Here I am, twenty years later, living proof that a daily renewal of one's relationship with God is the shortest distance between two points. It has affected every aspect of my life."

Questions for Reflection

- If a stranger approached you and wanted to talk to you about God, how would you react?
- What would influence you to listen to that person?
- What would influence you to brush the person off?

Jesus traveling throughout Galilee. Peter Maurin at the door. A young man backstage. Each of them challenged others to move beyond the routine, to do something special in the world. They were more than sounding boards reflecting stirrings in the souls of others. They were the ones who stirred up the souls, who lit the flame.

But the men and women of Galilee, Dorothy Day, and Noel Paul Stookey were not simply captivated by some magic spell woven by their mentors. They tested what these mentors stirred up against the hard realities of their daily lives and, out of that, found their calling.

[1]Day, Dorothy, *The Long Loneliness: An Autobiography*. New York: Harper & Row, 1981, paperback. Excerpt used with permission.

Four

A Family Tradition

Tobit thought he was near death.

Once he was a wealthy Israelite, but one who was also devout and generous and willing to take risks. "I would give my bread to the hungry and my clothing to the naked," Tobit tells us. "If I saw one of my people who had died and been thrown outside the walls of Nineveh, I would bury him" (Tobit 1:17).

But his life was not without its troubles. He had to curtail some of his purchasing trips because the roads became unsafe. He had to go into hiding when he incurred the wrath of the king for burying the bodies of slain Israelites. The king confiscated Tobit's property.

When a new king took the throne, Tobit regained his property, but then faced another misfortune. While he slept on the wall of his courtyard, bird droppings fell in his eyes and the cataracts they caused blinded him. After four years of blindness, Tobit was depressed, his marriage was strained, and he pleaded with God to take him:

> "For it is better for me to die
> than to endure so much misery in life,
> and to hear these insults!"
>
> Tobit 3:6

He called his son, Tobiah, to reveal where some of the family money was kept. He wanted Tobiah to go get the money so the

Family tradition can be
a way in which people
discover the call of God.

family could live well after his death. And he used the occasion to pass on to his son the values he held dear. He said:

"Honor your mother, and do not abandon her as long as she lives. . . .

". . . Perform good works all the days of your life, and do not tread the paths of wrongdoing. . . .

"Give alms from your possessions. Do not turn your face away from any of the poor, and God's face will not be turned away from you. . . .

"Be on your guard, son, against every form of immorality. . . .

"Do not keep with you overnight the wages of any man who works for you, but pay him immediately. . . . Do to no one what you yourself dislike. . . .

"Give to the hungry some of your bread, and to the naked some of your clothing. Whatever you have left over, give away as alms. . . .

"Seek counsel from every wise man, and do not think lightly of any advice that can be useful. At all times bless the Lord God, and ask him to make all your paths straight and to grant success to all your endeavors and plans."

Tobit 4:3-19

Tobit's is one of Scripture's most eloquent stories of family traditions being passed on from one generation to another. Family tradition, too, is another path through which people discern the call of God. (See Tobit 1-4.)

From our families, we learn ways to live out God's word. We see our parents pray and reach out to help others. We hear stories of relatives who give of themselves. We hear our parents as they tell us about their values and about their hopes for us. Then we try to make sense of it all. For some, that is the soil in which their call is rooted.

Questions for Reflection

- How were religious values passed on in your family?
- Have your ideas of religion and faith changed from those you were reared with?
- How are you passing on religious values to your children?

Bernie Juno grew up in a family in which religion was important.

She was one of five children in a Catholic family living in the central city of Milwaukee. She describes her upbringing as "very family oriented." Her father was active in their Catholic parish. Her mother was always there to help the neighbors.

"My family always reached out to other people and responded when they were called on," she said. "That was the biggest example — always being available."

Now Bernie does the same thing. She is director of Hebron House, a shelter for the homeless in Waukesha, Wisconsin — a city adjacent to the western boundary of Milwaukee County.

"I know what motivates me," she explained as she sat in the front-room office of the old home in downtown Waukesha. "It's my upbringing and my faith. Everything stems from that."

For thirteen years, Bernie worked as a dental hygienist. She taught religion classes at her church and helped out on the parish human concerns committee, but slowly her involvement began to deepen.

In 1977, a woman she knew asked her to help organize a dental clinic for the poor at St. Joseph's Parish in Waukesha. She agreed.

"The more you work in any of these areas, you recognize more and more what your neighbors are going through," she remembers. "Sometimes it's just too much. It calls you to action, and I guess that's what happened."

In 1983, she helped organize a Sunday meal program known as "Loaves and Fishes." That same year, Hebron House opened. It was named after the place where Abraham and Sarah met three strangers and extended hospitality to them. Hebron House now serves about fifty families a year. Bernie described its guiding philosophy this way: "Every person has dignity. They have a past and a future. What if that were me? What would I need to make me comfortable?"

Bernie said it is only in the past few years that she has developed a commitment to living a life of service.

"We all have gifts we can share with other people," she said. "I used to think my only gift was to be a good mother and wife and a good dental hygienist. Then I discovered that I had gifts to share with people. Part of that I discovered when I was asked.

"Somebody asked me to work on that dental clinic. I learned I had organizational skills and teaching skills and other skills that were needed to put something like that together. I think we have

Bernie Juno's call led
her to the discovery that
we all have gifts we can
share with other people.

to be called on before we can recognize those things in us."

Now Bernie Juno is trying to pass on her sense of service to her son and daughter, who are in their late adolescence. "I would hope that we are all teaching our children to do these things and not think that they are special or different," she said, echoing Tobit in a twentieth-century setting. "That's the way we live our lives — by helping someone else."

Question for Reflection

Bernie Juno recalled her father's activity in her parish and her mother's reaching out to neighbors. She drew some of her sense of call from what she saw her parents do while she was growing up.

• What kinds of things that you do now in the area of religion and service can you trace back to your family?

They came from very different backgrounds.

He grew up in Chicago, son of two bankers in a family that was only moderately religious.

She grew up in a small Kansas town, her life touched by the death of her mother in a family where religion played a central role.

Then their paths and their interests crossed. In college, they were both active in religious organizations that did work helping people. They met at a dance after a basketball game. They fell in love, got married, had four children, and struggled with ways to blend the worlds of religion, family, and work.

There was no dramatic moment of call for Bob and Mary Kay Bright. Their sense of vocation grew slowly over the years, affected by their own childhoods, their relationship with each other, and the people they met along the way. It is only in looking back that they can identify some of the touchstones that shaped God's call and their response.

Over the course of their lives, God's call has led them to work with Hispanic families trying to settle in the Madison, Wisconsin, area. It has brought them into deep involvement in education and social justice activities at the parishes they have been part of. It has propelled Bob into work to empower the poor and to battle discrimination. It has led Mary Kay to enrich the lives of older people with her presence. And it has guided them both as they tried to rear their children to share their beliefs and ideals.

Bob Bright is fifty now; Mary Kay is forty-eight. Their children are twenty-three, twenty-one, nineteen, and seventeen. They live in Oregon, Wisconsin, a village of 4,500 people about seven miles south of Madison. Their story is compelling not so much because of its drama, but more because they represent families who try to live out their call in the everyday settings of home, work, and parish.

Bob's interest in religion set him apart from the rest of his family. "I was always a religious kid," he recalls now. But he did not attend Catholic schools, and when he graduated from high school, he went to work as an insurance underwriter for a few years to earn money for college.

His parish priest suggested he go to St. Benedict College in Atchison, Kansas, about forty miles northwest of Kansas City. It was the early 1960s. "Here I was, this city slicker in the middle of Kansas," he says. It turned out to be the right place. One of the things that made it right was the Legion of Mary, a lay organization devoted to personal holiness and service to others.

There were seven or eight college men in the group, Bob remembers. "The guy in charge was very, very impressive to me, an older brother, role-model type," he says. "I'd never seen guys be religious and be involved in social activities, and I found that quite inspiring." He immersed himself in the group's activities, finding, for the first time, group support for his religious convictions, and encouragement to reach out to others through visits to jails and nursing homes. "That was my baptism," he says now.

Mary Kay, meanwhile, had followed a very different path to Mount St. Scholastica, the women's college that was also in Atchison.

The dominant event of her childhood was the sickness and death of her mother. "I was sort of never a child," Mary Kay explains. "I had a very strong sense of responsibility not only to my mother, but also to my little sister. From the time I was at least five, I had a very strong sense of taking care of other people."

She also had a strong sense of community support. Others in

Mary Kay and Bob Bright
discerned their call slowly,
drawing on moments
remembered from their
youth and on values
lived in their families.

Chanute, Kansas, a city of 10,000 in the southeastern corner of the state, rallied to help the family by, for example, taking the children on outings.

Her mother had cancer, an illness she battled for three or four years. She became a Catholic during those years. Mary Kay's father had attended a Jesuit college, and it was common for priests to be at their house.

When Mary Kay was nine, her mother died. "God has taken your mother to heaven," her father told her that New Year's Eve. Six months later, Mary Kay's grandmother, with whom they had lived for several years, died suddenly of a heart attack.

Her father remarried when she was twelve. Her stepmother had two younger children, so now Mary Kay was the oldest of four. She started going to a Catholic school.

There are memories from Mary Kay's childhood that helped shape her later life. She remembers in kindergarten befriending two classmates who were outcasts. She remembers, as a ten-year-old, practicing the organ in the big old church where both her parents had been baptized. There she developed a sense of the importance of sacred space. She remembers accompanying her grandmother — an Avon lady — on her rounds and learning to listen to older people talk.

By her high school years, her family had moved to Wichita, where she went to Mount Carmel Academy, a very strict girls' school. There she immersed herself in the sodality, a religious organization. As part of that organization's activities, each week she taught religion to children with Down's syndrome. "It was probably the first time in my life I was allowed to be very creative," she says, calling that experience "a real important stage in my development."

At Mount St. Scholastica, she majored in Spanish with a view toward becoming a teacher. She stayed active in sodality. And she danced with a kid from Chicago after a basketball game. "I was shocked at meeting someone from Chicago who was not a hoodlum," she recalls with a smile. They both went back to their dormitories that night and told their roommates they had met the person they would marry. They were right.

Mary Kay and Bob's common sense of religious activism prompted them to try to join the papal peace corps and go to work in British Honduras (now Belize) in Central America. But the bishop in charge of the program told them they had to be married for two years before they would be accepted. So Bob went to graduate school while Mary Kay cared for their first child.

It was a chaotic time in their lives as they moved to Champagne/Urbana, Illinois, to St. Louis, to Boston, and to Madison while Bob worked his way through graduate school in social work. Four babies and a miscarriage dominated Mary Kay's life. They were struggling with little money and career direction. "Planning was not part of our lives," she says.

By 1966 in Madison, though, the threads of their past began to form a tapestry of spirituality and action. They joined the Christian Family Movement at their parish, a movement whose hallmark was the slogan, "Observe, reflect, act."

The Brights met regularly with seven or eight other couples. Every time they met, a couple would report on actions they had taken. "That was very, very powerful," notes Bob. "Because it was the sixties, we were reflecting on a lot of things of our times. I found that very engaging."

For a brief time, they joined a floating Catholic community known as John XXIII. There, says Bob, "something started to happen that really changed our lives."

The community was working to help Hispanic families settle in Madison. The Brights grew close to one family. "We visited them every Sunday afternoon for five years," says Bob. "We were no longer volunteers. We were just friends."

"We were very, very inspired by this family," Bob says. And the experience helped pass a sense of call on to another generation. The Brights' oldest child, Laura, found that being with people who speak another language intrigued her. By the time she was a sixth grader, she was writing school papers about migrants. She retains a special interest in Latin America and has graduated from college with a degree in international management.

Mary Kay joined a mothers' group at the University Catholic Center, which helped her define the sense of call in her life. "It was a point at which I could sit down with other women and discuss the meaning of what we were doing then and in the future," she remembers.

Bob, meanwhile, found increasing ties between his faith and his work as a community organizer with the University of Wisconsin–Extension. "My work was very unusual in the kinds of circumstances it continuously presented to me," he acknowledges. He was called in as a mediator during racial disputes on campus. He worked with school dropouts from all backgrounds. He went

High school and college
activities can help shape our
awareness of God's call.

into prisons and halfway houses. He worked to urge churches to get involved in social policy. He was always involved with social change and conflict.

Underlying all his work was Bob's view of the value of each person, a view that he had gotten from his religion. And supporting his work was his regular attendance at the noonday Mass at the University Catholic Center. There, in the Gospel, he found support for his views; he had time to reflect on the day and on his life, and he refueled for the rest of the day. "That was the one way I felt I could be personal with the Lord," he says. "I don't think our church promotes that a lot. Doing that daily makes me feel like I am having a personal relationship."

In 1976, the Brights moved from a status-conscious section of Madison. Bob was uncomfortable with the materialistic values of the area. Mary Kay was tired of the pace of their urban lives. Their move to the rural village of Oregon opened up new opportunities for her.

She volunteered at a nursing home and found she could work well with very old and frail people. That led to a job as an outreach worker with the county commission on aging. She visited older people, helped them connect with local resources, and listened to their stories of life, faith, and death. Now she helps find employment for people over fifty-five.

Bob served on the village planning board, then was elected a village trustee. He chaired the parish council of their parish. And together, he and Mary Kay set out to develop an active social justice program for the parish. "Is it possible for a rural church to have peace and justice involvements?" asked Bob rhetorically. "The answer is a resounding yes."

Their parish now has nine groups underway, including a literature discussion group at a nearby prison, volunteers who assist at Madison meal and shelter programs, a blood donor group, visitors to the homebound, and volunteers who make tapes for the blind. All the groups are ecumenical, and all involve both men and women.

If the experiences of their youth helped shape Bob and Mary Kay, their life as a family has nurtured them in their sense of call. "We're real good at being open and communicative with each other," says Mary Kay. "We support each other at those times when you want to stop and give up."

They discerned their call slowly, drawing on moments from their youth and on their families' values. High school and college activities opened them to experiences they found meaningful.

48

Their marriage allowed them to support each other while remaining open to the needs of the community around them.

There were no voices in the night nor sudden conversions. No strangers dramatically altered their lives. By being attentive to the values of their lives, Bob and Mary Kay Bright have worked to live out their beliefs, following God's call at home, at work, and in their parish.

In some ways, family tradition extends beyond the immediate family. In the story of Tobit, the traditions were passed on explicitly. For Bernie Juno, they came from the example of her parents. For Bob and Mary Kay Bright, the family traditions grew out of a wide range of experiences they had while they were growing up. Their experiences involved family, school, neighbors, and friends. And for the Brights, the sense of call through family traditions extended into their marriage and their work as parents.

Families, then, can transmit God's call through the day-to-day moments of life, through the words of parents and the example they set. That should be no surprise. From the earliest stories in Scripture — Adam and Eve, Abraham and Sarah — to the story of Jesus' own growth, family often played a central role. It is still central today.

Question for Reflection

- What am I doing in my family to help my spouse and children or other relatives understand their own sense of God's call and develop ways to respond to that call?

Five

Mind and Soul

Nicodemus met Jesus in the world of ideas. In that meeting, in that exchange of ideas, Nicodemus was changed. He became a defender of Jesus in the councils of power; he came to honor Jesus after His death.

He was a Pharisee, a member of the Sanhedrin, an intellectual of Jerusalem. He was intrigued by what he had seen of Jesus and what he had heard of Him. Now, meeting Him under the cover of darkness, Nicodemus wanted to probe Jesus' ideas. They talked about being born of God, about being born again in the Spirit, about doing good deeds in the light. (See John 3:1-21.)

This is yet another way to figure out the direction of our lives — to struggle with the ideas that shape us and to test those ideas against our experience. These stories tell how three people discerned God's call through the life of the mind. They are people for whom reading and writing are important activities. They have taken the ideas they gleaned from their reading and their experience and used those ideas as a framework for their vocations.

Questions for Reflection

- What books that you have read have had a major impact on your thinking?
- Were these books novels, biographies, spiritual reading?
- Did any course you took in school help you in deciding the direction of your life?

Reading, discussion, and
experience opened new doors
for Jane Hammatt-Kavaloski
and Vince Kavaloski.

Vince Kavaloski's reading in his late grade school years was a little heavier than that of most pre-adolescents.

He was working on his grandfather's farm in Minnesota and reading Leo Tolstoy's *Anna Karenina*, the classic Russian novel.

That sparked Vince's interest in philosophy. "Philosophical issues are very much alive in Tolstoy's novels," he noted. To him, philosophy "seemed like the essence of life."

From that intellectual interest in philosophy, Vince has journeyed from traditional Catholicism to disillusionment with the Church to a rural Quaker community. For him, intellectual explorations of Socrates and Tolstoy are the bases of a life of activism built on faith.

Jane Hammatt-Kavaloski grew up in a crucible of activism — an urban slum in Dayton, Ohio. "I saw extreme poverty and violence as just a way of life," she recalled. "That left an imprint on me — residual fears that I don't think I can ever shake, but also a real commitment to righting those wrongs."

In the midst of the poverty and violence, her family tried to make their home a place of refuge. She remembers her mother seeking out a lonely elderly person to join them for Christmas or feeding the hoboes who came from the nearby railroad track. "I can't remember ever not thinking of doing social work," she said.

She worked her way through college, where she studied sociology and psychology. Then she went into the Peace Corps, serving two years in Morocco. That experience opened her eyes to the social structures that contribute to the problems of poverty and soured her on organized religion, as she watched some missionaries who were insensitive to the culture of the people they were trying to convert. Over time, though, she saw that religion had other dimensions as well.

Now, along with Vince, she runs the Ecumenical Partnership for Peace and Justice of the Wisconsin Conference of Churches. "We're attempting to retrieve the prophetic tradition," Jane said. Using biblical terms like *shalom, peace,* and *justice*, Vince added, "We're holding up a vision of what the world could be."

Theirs is a call that simmered over the years, a call shaped by intellectual searching and personal contact with people from many nations.

"The power of nonviolence runs through all of our presentations and all of our work," Vince explained. "It gives a concrete alternative to military or violent power, one that is consistent with the Judeo-Christian tradition as well as with the other great ethical systems the world has produced."

From his philosophical studies — he has a doctorate from the University of Chicago and teaches at the University of Wisconsin-Richland Center campus — Vince draws on the questions of Socrates: What is a just society? What do we have to do to move in that direction? From Socrates, he said, he has learned that "to be human is to be a citizen; to be a citizen is to be concerned about the common good and to see your own involvement in that common good."

In Tolstoy, he and Jane see a statement of the values that they share: a return to the land, a nonhierarchical community, resistance to state authority, a universal spiritual orientation.

And they see a common notion at the core of the world's religions: "We are all responsible for each other."

These beliefs have been thought through in an intellectual environment and tested in the Peace Corps and in the peace movement. They have been personalized through the couple's trips to the Soviet Union, Poland, and Central America. These beliefs, then, are the foundation for a life that is nurtured by a community on the land and animated by continuing efforts with church groups and others to work for peace and justice.

Vince and Jane now share their ideas with others through a newsletter and other writings. They try to touch the minds of their readers, and, in the process, they may open others to hearing God's call in new ways.

Questions for Reflection

The journey and current life of Vince and Jane may be different from those of many of us, but they offer an avenue to call worth exploring. For Vince and Jane, the power of ideas — sparked by reading and tested by discussion and experience — have opened new doors.

• What roles do reading and discussion play in your life?
• How can they help you test your sense of call?

Thomas Merton's discovery of his call is one of the most famous in this century. His 1948 autobiography, *The Seven Storey Mountain,* charted that discovery, and his later writings fleshed it out. He is now considered one of the giants of twentieth-century Catholic spirituality.

His call took him to a Trappist monastery, where he lived as a monk, one step removed from the secular world. Yet he still faced the same kinds of questions Christians face in the late twentieth century: Who is God? What role does God play in my life? What does God want me to do with my life?

Thomas Merton's discovery of his call began as an intellectual search. It changed him to the core of his being. It then involved a combination of a continued intellectual curiosity, a deep spiritual search, and a literary activism.

As the last in this series of reflections, Merton's story offers another lesson as well, a lesson about the need to re-examine one's calling and to adapt it to changing circumstances.

Merton had a transcontinental childhood. He was born in France and spent the early years of his life in Flushing, Long Island, New York. When he was six years old, his mother died. He then lived with his mother's parents outside New York City. His father, an artist, roamed the world and occasionally took Merton along.

When Merton was ten years old, he went back to France with his father. Three years later they moved to England. There, in 1931, when Merton was sixteen, his father died. He later described that as the year that left his soul absolutely devoid of any sense of religion.

The next year, an infection under a toenail turned into a full-blown case of blood poisoning. Merton thought he was going to die, but found no pleasure in survival. After his recovery, he went to Italy for a vacation, and there felt the first stirrings of a calling that would evolve over the next decade.

In Rome, he was captivated by the art in the Christian churches, and, through that art, he began to get some glimmer into the person of Christ. He bought a Bible and began to read the Christian Scriptures (New Testament). And then one night, alone in his room, he thought he sensed his father's presence. It was a transforming moment for Merton, a moment when he looked deep into his own soul, saw his failings, and began, for the first time in his life, to pray.

He hardly, however, became an instant monk. He came back

The graceful architectural lines
of medieval Christian churches
can inspire us to a deep faith.

to the United States to stay with his grandparents for a while, and he began to explore various religious traditions.

He returned to England in 1933 as a student at Clare College, Cambridge. Merton, however, was more playboy than scholar, enjoying both beer and women. After one year, his guardian sent him back to America and advised him not to return to Cambridge as a student. So he enrolled at Columbia University and directed his intellectual enthusiasm toward communism rather than Catholicism. But the courses at Columbia also began to awaken other parts of his intellect. Then, once again, deaths stirred his soul. A classmate died. His grandparents died. And again he became briefly — but seriously — ill.

One day in 1937, he bought *The Spirit of Mediaeval Philosophy*, a book by Etienne Gilson. He thought it would be a nice way to hearken back to his days in Europe. He was horrified to discover that it was a "Catholic book." But he read it.

In his book *Thomas Merton: A Pictorial Biography*, James Forest describes Merton's astonishment when he discovered parallels between Catholic theology and the graceful architectural lines of the churches he had admired in France and Italy.

Six months later, Merton read *Ends and Means* by Aldous Huxley — a book about mysticism in Christian and Eastern traditions, about pacifism, prayer, and asceticism. And then the mystical poetry of William Blake, an eighteenth-century Englishman, helped crystallize for Merton how central to one's life a living faith can be.

In August, 1938, Merton began attending Catholic Masses. And then, in the midst of reading a biography of Gerard Manley Hopkins, the Jesuit poet, Merton began to be bombarded with the urgency of the questions racing through his mind. Why wait, he kept asking himself in many different ways. He put down the book and sought out a priest who would help him become a Catholic. He was baptized on November 16, 1938.

But now what? He had hoped to become a writer, and he began working on novels. Merton was still restless, though. He talked to teachers and friends, and eventually, he decided to join the Franciscans — an order that Merton felt philosophically at home with. Once the Franciscans found out about Merton's wild past, however, they told him not to bother. He increased his private prayer life and joined a Franciscan movement for lay people. This movement was known as the Third Order. And when he registered for the draft in 1940 as the war in Europe grew

Through his books and
articles, Thomas Merton
shared his search for God.

more intense, he registered as a conscientious objector. But the army rejected him, too. He didn't have enough teeth.

Merton had heard about the Trappists, but he originally dismissed their life as too harsh. He even went so far as to tell a friend that he thought the harsh life of the Trappists would kill him. Nevertheless, he decided to spend Holy Week, 1941, at the Trappist Abbey of Gethsemani in Kentucky. He was impressed by what he found. "Could it possibly mean that I might someday become a monk in this monastery?" he wrote in his journal.

He feared another rejection. He decided to help with a clothing distribution project run by Friendship House, a lay Catholic project in Harlem. The results of racism became vivid to Merton. He saw a chance to do good work, and he felt the warm acceptance of the volunteer community and of the people they served.

On the night of November 27, Merton struggled with his call. Was that call to Harlem or to the Trappists? Whichever he chose, he would be following Christ. After much soul-searching, he decided to join the Trappists.

He entered the monastery on December 10, 1941. His intellectual journey continued, of course, leading him from embracing traditional Catholicism to being one of the voices of change that guided the Church through the turmoil of the 1960s. Merton, meanwhile, was reaching out to the East, stretching the bounds of his search for God. And through it all, he was sharing his journey with others through his books and articles, becoming a source for them to hear their calling even as he continually re-examined his own.

As he wrote in one essay, *Is the Contemplative Life Finished?*, "What each of us has to do and what I have to do is buckle down and really start investigating new possibilities in our own life; and if new possibilities mean radical changes, all right. Maybe we need radical changes for which we have to struggle and sweat some blood . . . but on the other hand, let these be real changes and not just neurotic upheaval."

And Merton knew that changes came even within one's calling. Colman McCarthy, the *Washington Post* columnist who spent five years in the Trappists in the 1960s, recalls members of his community in Georgia coming back from visits with Merton: "People have temporary vocations, Merton believed. This is one of the functions of the monastery — to be a type of graduate school where, instead of working on a thesis, you can work on yourself. If you have a vocation to the life, good; if not, that's all right, too.

You were generous to come and spend a few years trying it out. In the end, whether you work out your vocation here or in society, you should be remembered in this — you don't have a vocation, you are a vocation."

Questions for Reflection

Thomas Merton searched for a long time to find God and then to respond to God's call.

• What kind of religious searches have been part of your life?
• What has helped guide you through those searches?

Whether a call comes in the night or like a bolt out of the blue, whether it is inspired by friends or nurtured by family, whether it comes through years of reading or years of prayer — our task of listening to God and responding to the call never really ends. There may be a moment or a series of events or special people that help us discern our role in God's universe. But just as the universe evolves, that role is never static.

"You are a vocation," said Merton. The challenge for all of us is to discover the vocation that we are and then to live it out.

Wherever you are,
whatever you do,
you are a vocation.

NOTES

NOTES

NOTES